This is a gift for:

May these pages bring you comfort, peace,
and a gentle reminder that love never ends.

With love,

When Someone You Love Dies

True Stories That Bring Peace and Hope

Cynthia Zanetta Muir

This book is based on the personal experiences and perspectives of the author. It is intended to offer comfort, encouragement, and insight. It is not intended as medical, psychological, or professional advice.

Scripture quotations are from the Holy Bible.

Cover design by Debra Cloud

Dedication

This little book is dedicated to the one
who is missing someone deeply~
May these words bring comfort to
your heart, peace to your soul, and
a loving reminder that God is with you,
even at this very moment.

Hello, dear one,

If you are reading this, you have probably suffered a loss and I am so very sorry.

I, too, have lost people I love. I know the depth of impact it can have on your life.

It is never easy - whether you knew your loved one's time was coming, or it happened suddenly. It doesn't matter.

Loss is loss… and it hurts.

It can shake you to your very core.
It can knock you off balance.
It can make you feel as though a part of you is missing.

At times, it may feel like you can't go on… and yet somehow, you do.

You go through the motions.
You cry.
You feel alone.
Empty.

Numb.

It can feel like a loss of identity, because it is. If you were a wife, now you are a widow.

Your identity has changed. Maybe suddenly. And it takes time to acclimate to your new role.

My first loss was my only sister. I was a sister… and then, I wasn't. Loss changes something deep within you.

It really changes who you are.

And yet, as difficult as it is, we do begin to find our balance again. It may not seem like it right now, but you will eventually.

We are never quite the same after a loss, but we go on.

You may be doing well, then have a setback. You may have waves of grief that come unexpectedly, even when you thought you were doing better.

This is all part of the journey.

Death is a part of life, and we all know it.

Everyone dies. But when it touches someone we love, it can be extremely difficult. The Bible says a person's days are determined. Each of us has a number of days here, and then we are called home. But sometimes it feels untimely to us.

Everyone walks through grief differently. There is no set timeline for grief. But one thing remains the same:

God does not change. He loves you and He is the same, yesterday, today and tomorrow. In Psalm 34:18, we are reminded that:

"The Lord is near to the brokenhearted. And saves those who are crushed in spirit."

You are not alone.

When I was a young mother, I witnessed something, something that was miraculous. It changed how I saw death from the moment it happened.

I believe it was a gift from God. A gift I am meant to share with others. To bring another perspective, to enlighten.

When I speak to people about what I saw, it always brings comfort and peace. Every single time.

And now, I want to share this with you.

My prayer is that what you are about to read will stay with you and bring comfort and peace to your heart.

Millie's Story

Years ago, I experienced something that I have never forgotten. A monumental event in my life.

It was one of those moments that changes everything… even if you don't fully understand the value at the time.

When I was about 24 years old and a fairly new Christian, I attended the Tuesday morning Bible study for the ladies at my church. I loved it.

One Wednesday, the day after Bible study, I woke up early and couldn't stop thinking about Millie, my Bible study teacher. I didn't know her well enough to call her, but I felt compelled to pray for her. And I did, fervently.

That day I had a doctor's appointment about 30 miles away. As I was driving down the highway, just passing the exit to the hospital, a vision appeared in front of me. It was huge, like a drive-in movie screen. When it appeared, I was looking into a hospital room.

I recognized Millie standing with a woman next to a hospital bed. I somehow knew it was her mother. They were standing beside a man in the bed, who I instinctively knew was Millie's father.

I could see all the details in the room... the peachy colored walls, with wallpaper on the top half with peachy colored flowers. There was an empty bed in the room, the door to the hallway was closed, and the two women were quiet, standing side by side looking down at her father.

Suddenly a man appeared on the foot of the bed. He was brilliant and glowing, and light was emanating from him. I immediately recognized him to be Jesus.

Jesus stood elevated on top of the end of the bed, dressed in a long white robe. He was illuminated at the same time. He bent over slightly and extended his arms out to Millie's father. At that moment, I saw her father's spirit rise up out of his body into the outstretched arms of Jesus, and he was embraced by the Lord. It was surreal.

Tears poured down my face. Watching this was so emotional and it felt both solemn and sacred.

I realized that Millie's father had died and at that instant something strange happened. I could feel what Millie was feeling… a warm peace and comfort, a strength from God came into her to comfort her at that moment.

Then the vision in front of me faded, and everything went away. I thought, *Wow! What was that?*

I knew this was significant, but what did it mean? Was Millie's father going to die? I didn't know and I kept this vision to myself.

The following Sunday I heard at church that Millie's father had passed away that week. I thought, *Whoa! It really happened.* I was a little shaken, but I still didn't say anything to anyone.

On Tuesday I went to the Bible study as I usually did because I did not miss Tuesday morning. It was the highlight of my week. On the way, I talked to God and asked for a confirmation from Him. If He wanted me to tell Millie about the vision, I needed to be alone with her. I was nervous about telling her for some reason, so I wanted a sign from God.

I thought there wouldn't be a chance to be alone with her since there was usually about 20 women in a small house. It would be the sign that I needed.

When I got to the Bible study, the living room was already full of women and Millie was sitting in her chair, about ready to start. I put my purse and Bible down in the living room and walked into the kitchen to grab a cup of coffee. I was the only one in the kitchen as I poured my coffee and added some cream. With cup in hand I turned to walk out of the room, but Millie came walking through the door before I took two steps. I took a deep breath, feeling slightly anxious because of my promise to God. It was obviously a sign to tell her.

I said in a soft voice, "Millie, I was sorry to hear about your father. I have something I want to share with you."

Millie responded, "You do?" And looked at me inquisitively, giving me her full attention at that moment. "Yes I do and I think it might be important to you," I said.

I began to tell her. "Last Wednesday morning, I felt compelled to pray for you and it seemed like I couldn't stop. I was praying for you all morning and even after I left my house to go to the doctor, I was still praying for you."

I continued, looking straight into her eyes, "As I was driving down the highway, a vision appeared in front of me. It was you and your mom standing by your dad in the hospital." Millie took a step closer as she was listening to every word. "You were praying for me on Wednesday? What was the vision?"

Before I spoke, I thought about how to best describe what I saw, because I hadn't told anyone. As I began to speak, the words flowed out of me. "It was like a huge drive-in theater screen up in the air in front of me as I was driving. And it was clear. I could see you and your mother standing in a hospital room next to a bed. I could see a man lying on the bed and I knew it was your father."

As I was describing the hospital scene, Millie was nodding her head up and down, listening intently to every word I spoke. She kept nodding so I continued, "I could see the whole room. I saw an empty bed behind you and your mother. The room was kind of a peachy color, and half of the wall was wallpapered with peachy colored flowers."

Millie's eyes got bigger as I described the room in detail. She responded enthusiastically, "There *was* an empty bed! I *was* with my mother! It was only the two of us with my father. The room had peachy colors on the wall! You are describing the room *exactly* as it was!" She was in awe.

"I haven't told you the best part yet, Millie," I said with a slight smile. She was captivated and hanging on every word now. "I saw Jesus standing on the foot of the bed. He extended His arms towards your father, and I saw your father's spirit leave his body and rise up to be embraced by Jesus!"

As I told her, I was showing her with my hands how her father's spirit rose up. Millie's eyes began to well up with tears as she nodded in agreement once again, and she said, "That helps me, it gives me insight, because right before my father died, it seemed like he was struggling for a moment. Something was happening but I couldn't understand. After hearing this, I believe he saw Jesus standing there. He wanted to be with Him."

After seeing Millie's reaction, I was so glad I told her. "Thank you so much for sharing this with me," she said graciously. "This means so much to me to hear Jesus was there when my father died. It's wonderful you saw this vision!"

I nodded again, feeling grateful that she was blessed by hearing about it. I think she knew I was a little nervous when I was telling her.

I felt relieved because I didn't know how she would respond. I was so young and naive about many things and had not put it all into the right perspective until then. As I was leaving the room, she said,

"Wait. I have one more question for you." I stopped and turned around to look at Millie. She asked, "What time did this happen on Wednesday?" A curious look came on her face.

I thought about it for a moment and said, "It would have been about 12:15."

She responded with a look of surprise and said, "That's exactly what time he died!"

I was stunned! When I heard those words, chills went down my spine. I was shocked! I actually witnessed her father die as it was happening.

I didn't know what to think. This seemed weird, like "woo-woo" weird, but I knew it was significant and I knew God orchestrated this whole thing.

I felt led to ask Millie if she could describe to me how she felt immediately after her father died. She said, "It was as if God came into me and gave me strength and comfort, in my inner being. I felt the warmth of God and He gave me such peace." I nodded my head, acknowledging what she had just shared.

"I was wondering about that because it was like I could feel what you were feeling, but I didn't know if it was even possible," I told her.

We both looked at each other, and there was a pause as we considered what God had done. I think we were both amazed at that moment.

This was a surprising conversation for both of us. Everything about this experience was supernatural. We set our coffee cups down on the table and hugged a long hug, and she thanked me again.

It wasn't until I was walking out of the kitchen that another woman came in to get something. Millie and I had a private time together undisturbed by anyone. I believe God set this special time apart for us in a house full of women.

From time to time I wondered why God showed this vision to me. Why Millie's father? It was such a personal moment in their lives for me to witness.

Millie's parents lived out of town, and I didn't know them. But with God, nothing is by accident.

My Father

I was very close to my father. He was a gentle, loving man, who held strong beliefs that family comes first before anyone or anything else.

Several months after Millie's father passed away, my father was diagnosed with aggressive lymphoma.

He went from being a healthy working man to being bedridden and unable to walk in less than six months. He was only 48.

I remember sitting next to him one day, and we were talking for the longest time about God and Heaven. He looked up at me, his eyes locked on mine, and a tear rolled down his cheek, "Even though I'm withering away, I know God is with me, and I know where I'm going."

My father told me I had to let him go. And even though his body was only skin and bones, I didn't want to let him go. He thought my prayers were keeping him alive. We had such an emotional conversation that day. I didn't want to lose my father. But he was ready to leave this world. He wanted permission to go.

In his final moments, my mother and I stood side by side next to his bed in the hospital. There was an empty bed in the room. The door was closed to the hallway. Same situation, different place.

His breathing was labored, he had a blank look in his eyes, almost glazed over it seemed. The doctor had just left the room telling us that he didn't have much time. "Minutes," he said.

As my mother and I stood there, we were encompassed by the heaviness waiting for the inevitable to happen. We didn't say a word. We watched my father's chest rise and fall as he struggled with each breath he took.

Suddenly, he clinched his eyes – closing them tightly. When he opened them, his eyes were clear. He looked straight up at me and winked one eye dramatically, and then he winked the other eye. Then he smiled… and that was his last breath.

I knew my father well. He was communicating and he didn't want there to be any mistake about it. He winked twice because he wanted to make sure we knew he was winking at us, to tell us everything was okay. He was telling us in the only way he could at that moment.

As soon as the life left his body, I felt that warm comfort and peace come into me that I felt when Millie's father died. I recognized that same peace I did that day I saw the vision. I could feel the presence of God in the room, and I knew at that moment what was happening…

My father was being embraced by the Lord!

That's when I remembered Millie's story.

It wasn't until that moment, that I realized God, in His graciousness, was preparing me for this.

God comforted Millie, He comforted me, and I know He will comfort you. Matthew 5:4 says:

"Blessed are those who mourn for they shall be comforted."

What Really Happens

Death is the Doorway

When we lose someone we are left without them.

We may suffer because we don't have them with us.

And the moments we shared are now memories.

Even so, I believe what Paul said in 2 Corinthians 5:8:

"To be absent from the body is to be in the presence of the Lord."

And I saw it happen in real time.

Let's consider a different perspective…

There are now millions of accounts from around the world of people who have had what are called near-death experiences - moments where they were clinically gone yet returned to life, with vivid memories of what they encountered.

Many describe being surrounded by the greatest love they have ever felt. They talk about seeing loved ones who had gone before them… sometimes they saw their beloved pets.

Many describe seeing vivid colors, more intense, more beautiful than any on earth. The flowers and the trees are more alive than they've ever seen here. "It's far more real than earth," is often reported… "and more beautiful than you can ever imagine."

So many say they felt like they were "home."

So much so that many did not want to return. But they were told, "It's not your time… you have to go back."

When they return, they are profoundly changed. Their faith in God shifts from belief… *to knowing.*

These people lose all fear of dying.

Their understanding of life is transformed.

After having these heavenly experiences, they say the same thing: that what matters most in this life is love – and being kind to others.

These accounts don't replace faith…
but they echo what faith has always pointed to:

God is real.
Heaven is real.
And this life is not the end of our story.

Can you imagine your loved one being welcomed by Jesus as they passed from this life and into His arms?

Can you imagine the joy they felt seeing loved ones and family members who got there before them?

From our perspective, it's hard not to have them here… but from their perspective, they are now "home."

In a place more wonderful, more alive, and filled with more love than we can ever fully comprehend.

Paul understood this perspective.

That Heaven *is* the goal. He saw it as the grand reward for going through this life, and the pains and suffering he went through. It's like winning a prize the way Paul explains it. You can't lose - if you stay on earth, it's for God, and if you leave, you are *with* God.

Paul said in Philippians 3:14:

"I press on toward the goal for the prize of the upward call of God in Christ Jesus."

What if the moment we call loss… was the moment they experienced the greatest joy of their life?

There truly is a reality beyond what we see.

A promise that life does not end - it continues.

And while we remain here, walking through days that sometimes feel heavy with absence… our loved ones are not walking in absence at all.

They are whole.
They are alive.
They are in the presence of love that surpasses anything we have known.

And one day… what now feels like separation will be revealed as only a moment in time.

Dear One,

May you know the joy of the Lord in this season. For the joy of the Lord is truly your strength.

May these words settle deep within your heart as you walk forward with quiet assurance that your loved one is in the presence of the Lord – alive, whole, and surrounded by love – and those loved ones who arrived before them.

This perspective may feel new, even difficult to embrace at first. But as your heart begins to receive it, you may find that it gently softens your grief and brings peace to your days.

Though you miss them, you can rest in the truth that you will see them again.

God is with you. His word says He is near to the brokenhearted. May His presence surround you and lift you up, and may He guide you through this season. **You are not alone.**

Reflecting on Perspective

From this side,
it feels like loss.

From the other side,
it's an arrival.

Sit with this thought a moment...
your loved one is in the most
wonderful place.

And one day,
you will be reunited.

Psalm 23

The Passion Translation

1 The Lord is my best friend and my shepherd.

I always have more than enough.

2 He offers a resting place for me in His luxurious love.

His tracks take me to an oasis of peace, the quiet brook of bliss.

3 That's where He restores and revives my life.

He opens before me pathways to God's pleasure and leads me along in His footsteps of righteousness so that I can bring honor to His name.

4 Lord, even when Your path takes me through the valley of deepest darkness, fear will never conquer me, for You already have!

You remain close to me and lead me through it all the way.

Your authority is my strength and my peace.

The comfort of Your love takes away my fear.

I'll never be lonely, for You are near.

5 You become my delicious feast

even when my enemies dare to fight.

You anoint me with the fragrance of Your Holy Spirit; You give me all I can drink of you until my heart overflows.

6 So why would I fear the future?

For Your goodness and love pursue me all the days of my life.

Then afterward, when my life is through,

I'll return to Your glorious presence to be forever with You!

May these words remind you that no matter the season…

God's love and presence are unshakable.

Trust in Him, lean into His promises, and let His peace fill you, comfort you, and give you hope.

A Gift for You

If these words have brought you comfort, I would like to share something more with you.

A couple of days after the passing of my husband, I wrote what felt like a letter from heaven.

The words came to me line by line. It brought me such a deep sense of peace.

Many who have read this, read it again and again. It is very comforting and gives affirmation to the wonders of Heaven.

If you would like to receive the "Letter from Heaven" as a free gift, you can find it here: cynthiazmuir.com/gift

May it bring comfort and peace to your heart.

www.ingramcontent.com/pod-product-compliance
Ingram Content Group UK Ltd.
Pitfield, Milton Keynes, MK11 3LW, UK
UKHW042019290726
14061UKWH00002BB/92

9 798995 784500